More

IF YOU HAD TO CHOOSE,

What Would You Do?

"This is a MUST read. Sandra Humphrey has honed her writing skills to a sharp edge. *More If You Had to Choose, What Would You Do?* challenges our young people to reach inside themselves, to ponder, to explore their moral fiber—to examine who they are and who they are becoming."

Dr. Terry Hitchcock
Executive Director, Heroes & Dreams Foundation

"Sandra Humphrey highlights for kids the kinds of decisions they are called on to make in everyday life. It is not always easy to live what we believe, but her book provides an easy and fun way to give young people practice in choosing to 'do the right thing' in the face of peer pressure and self-interest."

Sr. Maria Grace Dateno, FSP
Editor, *My Friend—The Catholic Magazine for Kids*

"Sandra Humphrey presents very real moral situations in her new book that prepare kids to make responsible choices and guess who wins? Kids! Their parents! All of us!"

Gene Bedley, PTA National Educator of the Year

"Sandra Humphrey has provided a valuable resource for concerned educators, parents, and students. Through a series of well-developed, interesting, and true-to-life scenarios, Ms. Humphrey poses profound questions involving such issues as peer relationships, academic integrity, and personal responsibility. Each piece will facilitate a lively discussion and will help young people assess the potential consequences of their actions. When armed with awareness and knowledge, students will be able to make informed, intelligent choices when confronted with the complex dilemmas of our modern society and through wise decisions achieve happiness and success in both their scholastic and personal lives."

Philip Bigler, Director, The Madison Center
James Madison University

"I wish I'd had a book like this when I was a young person growing up. These well-crafted short stories, all open-ended, draw young readers into challenging situations with the invitation to write their own endings. One value for young readers is the fact that all of these stories are based on situations that happen to youngsters everywhere."

Michael L. Sherer
Editor, *Metro Lutheran* newspaper

More
IF YOU HAD TO CHOOSE,
What Would You Do?

Sandra McLeod Humphrey

ILLUSTRATED BY BRIAN STRASSBURG

Sandra McLeod Humphrey

PB Prometheus Books

59 John Glenn Drive
Amherst, New York 14228-2197

Published 2003 by Prometheus Books

Inquiries should be addressed to
Prometheus Books, 59 John Glenn Drive, Amherst, New York 14228–2197.
VOICE: 716–691–0133, ext. 207.
FAX: 716–564–2711.
WWW.PROMETHEUSBOOKS.COM

07 06 05 04 03   8 7 6 5 4

Interior design by Jacqueline Cooke
Illustrated by Brian Strassburg

Library of Congress Cataloging-in-Publication Data

Humphrey, Sandra McLeod.
    More if you had to choose, what would you do? / Sandra McLeod Humphrey ; illustrated by Brian Strassburg.
        p. cm.
    Summary: Presents a number of scenarios involving ethical dilemmas and asks the reader to decide what to do.
    ISBN 1-59102-077-8 (pbk. : alk. paper)
    1. Ethics—Juvenile literature. 2. Children—Conduct of life. [1. Conduct of life. 2. Ethics.] I. Strassburg, Brian, ill. II. Title.

BJ1631.H86   2003
170—dc21   2003041259

Printed in the United States of America on acid-free paper

*Dedicated to young people everywhere
and to those who care about them.*

Contents

Author's Note Do you try to do what you know is right even when no one is watching? It's not always easy, is it?

Especially when your friends are telling you to do something else. Or maybe the decision is a really tough decision or you're not even sure what the right decision is.

Just as we build up our bodies by exercising our physical muscles, we also need to build strong moral muscle by learning to make good choices in difficult situations.

Life is all about choices. How and what we choose can determine not only our character but also the quality of our life. As they say, "Practice makes perfect." So read through the twenty-six stories in this book and exercise your "moral muscle" at the same time.

Pretend you are in each situation and practice making choices—good choices. The more you practice now, the more prepared you'll be later on to make the right choices when you find yourself in difficult situations.

Most of the stories are about moral issues, but some of the stories will also get you thinking about important life principles such as how we treat other people, how we deal with peer pressure, and how we decide what "being cool" really means.

Reading the stories with others and talking about the questions at the end of each story can be fun, too. Sometimes sharing your ideas with other people can help you to understand better the choices you make and how you make them.

Now, last but most important: Whether you read this book alone or with others, I hope you enjoy it the same way you would enjoy a good friend!

Been There, Done That!

I wish I could erase last week from from my life! That's when Ms. Porter dropped her bomb.

Don't get me wrong here, I love social studies. Ms. Porter is probably my favorite teacher, and I always look forward to doing our group projects every spring.

Correction: I used to look forward to doing them until she wrecked my whole life by changing the rules.

I had everything all planned. I was going to partner up with Tim and Nick again as usual. We made a great team and we always ended up getting an A+ on our projects.

But this year Ms. Porter decided that *she* was going to choose our project partners for us and that's how I, Andy Sadowsky, ended up with Ty Rafferty and Jon McKenzie.

On Monday, when she dropped the bomb, I was not a happy camper, but I was going to try to bite the bullet and make the best of a bad situation.

11

So after school, when I spot Ty and Jon by the water fountain, I plaster a smile on my face and jog on over there.

Ty would be pretty hard to miss in his bright neon green sweat suit with matching socks. And I can hear Jon's scratchy voice loud and clear from twenty feet away.

So I ask the guys if they have any ideas for our group project yet. Jon grins and points to a poster of Mexico taped to the wall next to the school cafeteria.

"I was just trying to talk Ty here into doing our social studies report on Mexico City. You know, like a virtual vacation. We could get a ton of stuff off the computer and—"

"But we've already done that," Ty interrupts. "We did a virtual trip to Brazil last year. Besides, that report was too much work. I spent hours on the computer just digging up stuff about Brazil."

That's when I know I've got a problem. Good grief, Tim and Nick and I spent *weeks* at the library digging up info on the rain forests. We practically lived and breathed nothing but rain forests the whole time.

"But we got a B– on that report," Jonathan protests, "and this would be a whole different country. What do you think, Andy?"

"How about something on endangered animals?" I toss out, crossing my fingers at the same time.

Ty makes his eyeballs roll all the way up in his head, so all you can see are the whites, and groans. "No way, man, I've already done stuff like that."

So I try again. "What about doing a science experiment?"

Ty sticks his finger down his throat and pretends to gag.

"I don't think so! We spent all last year doing experiments in our science class and I'm full up to here." He draws his hand across his chest for extra emphasis.

I can feel my stomach beginning to churn, but I'm not ready to give up. So I keep tossing out ideas while each one gets shot down. Either one of the guys has already done something like it or it's "too much work."

I'm still hanging in there tossing out ideas when Ty lets loose with a double-fingered whistle and signals for a time-out. "I say we just do the the easiest thing we can, like maybe a biography of someone like Abraham Lincoln. We read a few pages, we write a few paragraphs, and we're done! What do you say?"

Jon shoots Ty a thumbs-up while I'm trying to keep from barfing.

So where does that leave me? Either I slide by with the minimum like the other guys or else I do most of the work myself, so that we end up with a decent report.

If you were Andy, what would *you* do? Why?

More to think about:

Why do you think Ms. Porter assigns the group project every year?

Why do you think Ms. Porter decided to choose the teams this year rather than allowing students to form their own teams?

Why do you think she paired Andy with Ty and Jon?

Do you think it's fair if Andy ends up doing all the work?

Do you know kids who try to just "slide by" with the minimum?

What do you think Andy will end up doing? Why? How do you think he will feel about the choice he makes?

Can you think of any other options for Andy?

Not Exactly

"So what's happening, dude?" Daniel asked, as he plopped down on Zachary's bed.

Zachary held up a sheet of paper and grinned. "I'm starting my report for social studies. You know, how we're supposed to write about what a real friend is. Do you want to hear what I've got so far?"

Daniel leaned back and rested his head against Zachary's huge football pillow. "Sure, shoot, man. I'm all ears."

"Okay, I start out by saying that you can always count on a real friend to stick by you no matter what. Especially during the bad times. Do you remember last summer when I struck out three times in a row and all the guys got on my case? I felt like it was my fault that our team didn't make it into the playoffs, and I was even thinking about not signing up for base-ball this summer."

Daniel grabbed his throat and made a gagging sound. "How could I forget! You were really bad, man. You hit a few singles, but that was one long, dry summer!"

Zachary nodded. "I know. I couldn't ever seem to connect with the ball. It was just one strike after another. But, in spite of how bad I was, my best friend never got on my case. He never told me what a loser I was or blamed me for messing up."

Daniel popped his bubble gum and blew a huge bubble. "So who is this best friend you're talking about? Coach Williams? He never got down on you even when you missed that easy fly ball."

Zachary shook his head. "Not exactly. I like Coach Williams a lot, but he's not my best friend. Let me tell you some more about my best friend and see if you can guess who he is."

Daniel reached for the model airplane on the nightstand next to the bed and let out a huge sigh. "Okay, man, I'm ready. Give me another clue."

Zachary glanced down at his paper. "My best friend cares more about my insides than my outsides."

Daniel stopped popping bubbles and frowned. "So what does that mean?"

"It means that my best friend doesn't care what I wear or how many video games I have. He cares more about what I'm like on the inside. Whether I think for myself or whether I just do what everyone else does. Are you ready to guess yet?"

Daniel shook his head. "For a minute I thought I was, but give me another clue first."

Zachary picked up his pencil and wrote some more. "I think it's important for best friends to be honest with each other and I know that I can tell my best friend anything."

Daniel twirled the propeller on the model airplane and then watched it slowly spin to a stop.

"It's got to be your grandfather. You can tell him anything."

Zachary stopped writing and put his pencil down. "Not exactly. Okay, I'll give you one last clue. Remember when I first transferred to your school two years ago? I was a new kid and nobody likes new. I had nobody to hang out with and I was feeling kind of like an alien from another galaxy."

Daniel spun the propeller again and winced. "I remember. You didn't say two words that whole first week. For a while, we all thought maybe you couldn't talk. Or maybe you didn't know any English. That's why I invited you to my pizza party, and look at us now. We're so tight, you couldn't pry us apart with a pizza cutter."

Zachary nodded. "I guess I was kind of a dweeb back then. So, anyway, have you figured out who my best friend is yet?"

Who do *you* think Zachary's best friend is? Why?

More to think about:

What is a real friend?

Do you think a real friend accepts you just as you are? Why or why not?

Can you have lots of friends and still be lonely? Why or why not?

Do you care more about your friends' "insides" or "outsides"?

What character traits would you want your best friend to have?

Too Close to Call

The race for class president was close. Too close for comfort. Sam wasn't worried about Clark or Ryan, but he *was* worried about Heather.

Heather was new this year, but that hadn't stopped her from running a really aggressive campaign. She seemed to be everywhere these days.

In the morning she was at the front door shaking hands with just about every kid in the school, not just the kids in their class.

At noon she was always in the cafeteria handing out flyers. And, of course, shaking hands again.

And after school she was always out on the soccer field checking out possible voters she might have missed.

She even stopped by the band room while Sam was rehearsing his clarinet solo for the school concert to leave more flyers. Somehow it didn't seem right that she should leave flyers in the band room when she didn't even play an instrument.

There were only two weeks to go and she was winning more votes by the day. Maybe by the hour.

After he put his clarinet away, Sam picked up one of Heather's flyers to see what he was really up against.

He already knew most of the stuff: honor roll, science club, chess club, volunteer tutor for kids in one of the "special classes," a community service award. . . . The list seemed to go on forever.

There was no way he could win the election when he was running against Supergirl!

But on Friday afternoon at 3:00 everything changed! That's when Sam learned something new about Heather.

That's when one of his friends on the track team delivered some news that could guarantee an election win for Sam.

Sam found out that Heather had been suspended last year from her old school for smoking on the school grounds. He couldn't believe it! Supergirl Heather had actually been suspended.

What a bonanza! It looked like he was back in the race again for real. All he had to do was spread the news around the school and he could stop worrying about the election.

Wasn't that the way the real politicians did it? Win at any cost! Maybe so, but was it *his* way?

He knew what his buddies would say. They would tell him to go for it! Chad had even offered to tell all the guys on the track team, and he knew that Rick would see to it that everyone on the basketball team knew.

But then Sam thought about Heather again. Why was this election so important to her? What was she trying to prove?

She had worked hard to make a fresh start at a new school. Would it be right for him to make a big thing out of one past mistake just to win an election?

He wondered what she would do if she were in his place. Would she dig up his past and use it to her advantage? He didn't really know, but it wasn't her decision anyway. It was his, and he didn't have a lot of time to think about it with the election less than two weeks away.

As he passed the bulletin board next to the gym, he saw one of her flyers tacked up there next to the track schedule.

Heather's face was smiling back at him like she didn't have a care in the world. Well, he could change all that in no time.

He knew now that he could destroy the competition and win the election with no sweat. But how would he feel if he won the election by attacking his opponent's character?

He really wanted to win the election, but at what cost?

If you were Sam, what would *you* do? Why?

More to think about:

Why do you think Heather changed schools?

Why do you think winning this election is so important to her?

What do you think will happen to Heather if Sam reveals her suspension at her old school?

How do you think Sam will feel if he wins the election by revealing Heather's past mistake?

How important is winning? Does it really matter *how* we win?

Collision Course

"So are you going to do it or not?" Shelly demanded, locking her blue eyes on me.

I shook my head and pried a dill pickle out of the jar. "I don't know. It just isn't right."

She stopped spreading peanut butter on her bread and heaved a huge sigh. "Andrea, sometimes you are such a pain! Don't you want to be part of the in-group for once in your life, instead of always being an outsider? Tara and Lindsay have already done it."

Shelly snapped her fingers. "Just like that, they're in."

I stopped munching on my pickle and shook my head again. "It's still shoplifting and it's still wrong."

Shelly put her knife down and glared at me. "Shoplifting is taking something important, like clothing or jewelry. All we have to do is steal a stupid banana from Mr. Stein's deli. One banana. Do you hear me? *One* measly banana!"

I put my pickle down on my plate and opened a bag of corn chips. "Even if it's just a single toothpick, it's still stealing."

I watched Shelly's ears turn red and her face scrunch up. I knew what was coming.

"Andrea," she finally said, "we have been best friends since first grade, but we'll be going into junior high next year and you're still acting like some goody-goody first grader. You've got to get with it or we're always going to be outsiders, just watching everyone else have all the fun."

She took a breath while I waited for what I knew was coming. "Andrea, if you don't do this with me, then I'll do it alone, but I'm doing it with or without you!"

For weeks I had known that I was on a collision course with my best friend. "I'm sorry, but I just don't think I can," I finally managed to mumble, over the chip stuck in my dry throat and the butterflies whirling around in my stomach.

Shelly stared at me like I'd totally lost all my marbles. "Andrea, you can't be serious. Who is going to get hurt? Will Mr. Stein really miss a couple pieces of fruit? Will he go bankrupt because we take two stupid bananas? Who is ever even going to know what we did?"

"I would know," I said, staring into my bag of corn chips.

"You are just so seriously uncool," Shelly groaned, grabbing her backpack and slinging it over her shoulder. "I just don't think I can hang out with you anymore."

Then she stormed out of the kitchen, banging the screen door behind her.

It wasn't like I didn't know this moment was coming. I had been expecting it since the beginning of the year when Shelly began hanging out with new kids, different kids.

Kids like Collin, who admitted right up front that he cheated on his math test. Not only did he admit it, he was proud of it. He claimed that anyone who wanted to get anywhere these days had to cheat and that everybody did it. When he explained how he had done it, all his friends told him how cool he was.

If I ever tried cheating like that, I'd be throwing up halfway through the test, my brain would experience a total meltdown, and my hands would be shaking so much I wouldn't be able to write down my answers, even if I knew them.

And then I remembered how Randall had called in to school, pretending to be his dad. He told Mrs. Preston, the office secretary, that his son was sick and wouldn't be coming to school that day.

All of Shelly's new friends thought what Randall did was totally awesome and everybody was high-fiving him like he was a real hero. All I could think about was, what if he got caught? What then?

Maybe Shelly was right. I had to admit I was definitely uncool if being cool meant being able to lie and cheat and break rules without feeling guilty.

If you were Andrea, what would *you* do? Why?

More to think about:

Do you think Shelly's new friends are "cool"? Why or why not?

Are these friends you would want to have? Why or why not?

Do your friends sometimes try to pressure you to do something you don't want to do? What do you do?

What does "being cool" mean to you?

How could Shelly and Andrea reach such completely different decisions about taking fruit from Mr. Stein's market?

Declaration of War

Uncle Arthur left me no choice. I had to declare war. It was a matter of honor—mine.

Now don't get me wrong. I'm basically your nice generic kind of kid. I don't stick my used chewing gum under my desk at school. I don't spit in the water fountain at the movies. And I even remember to feed the birds.

I did feel really bad when Aunt Ellie died. And then, as if that wasn't bad enough, Uncle Arthur's dog Mortimer died, too. But that was still no reason for Uncle Arthur to steal my room.

To be fair, I guess it wasn't really my uncle's idea to steal my room. It was my mom's.

I still remember her exact words: "It won't be forever, Jason. Just a few weeks, maybe a month or so. Just till Uncle Arthur begins feeling better."

Well, I've got news. It's been over two months and Uncle Arthur still has my room and I'm still stuck in Mom's little sewing room.

Right now I'm lying in bed staring at the ceiling because I do my best thinking when I'm staring at the water spots on the ceiling.

And I have decided as of this very moment that enough is enough. I'm declaring war on Uncle Arthur.

What I need first is an objective. You can't plan anything, especially a war, without an objective. In this case, my objective is to make Uncle Arthur's life here so miserable that he will *want* to leave. Then I'll get my room back and life will get back to normal for all of us.

My next step is a battle plan. You can't just declare war on someone without a plan of action.

So now I've got to make a big decision. Do I let Uncle Arthur know that I've declared war on him or do I resort to guerrilla warfare? It's a big decision, so I've got to do some serious thinking here.

What I need is some sugar to get my creative juices flowing, so I pull on some jeans and a T-shirt and head down to the kitchen to get a bowl of Sugar Doodles.

Did I mention that Uncle Arthur has also stolen my dog? Well, he has. At this very moment, my uncle and Mac are out taking their morning walk. They have been taking long walks together every day and Uncle Arthur even takes Mac fishing with him.

While I'm pouring the Sugar Doodles into a bowl, I'm thinking guerrilla tactics are the way to go. That way I can do a lot of little stuff and not have to resort to anything too radical.

But by the time I've poured myself a glass of milk, I'm remembering how Uncle Arthur helped me give Mac a bath last week, which is no small job since Mac weighs in at over a hundred pounds.

And while I'm buttering my toast, I'm remembering how Uncle Arthur taught me how to fish when I was just a little kid. I still have the picture he took of me and my eight-pound walleye on the shelf next to my bowling trophy.

By the time I'm crunching away on my last Sugar Doodle I'm remembering all the great baseball games we've gone to together and how he always buys me all the chili dogs I can eat.

Sure, I want my room back, but I think I would really miss Uncle Arthur a lot if he weren't here. And I think Mac would miss him a whole lot, too.

If you were Jason, what would *you* do? Why?

More to think about:

How do you think Uncle Arthur felt after Aunt Ellie died?

What do you think he needs to help him feel better?

Which do you think are more important: people or things? Why?

Can you think of a solution to Jason's problem where everyone can come out a winner?

Instant Replay

Brianna took a deep breath and counted to ten. This time she had really had it with Jillian. Enough was enough!

Jillian always had to be first in everything: the highest grade on every math test, first place in every gymnastic tournament, and even first in the lunch line.

She had been that way since the first grade and every year since then it had been just more of the same.

If Jillian didn't score the most points in every volleyball game, she blamed Coach Harper for not letting her play longer.

And when she didn't get the starring role in the class play, she refused to take any other role. She also refused to paint scenery or work on the lighting or do anything else.

The other kids were beginning to drop Jillian like a hot potato. They all agreed that she was just not a team player.

Brianna was about the only friend Jillian had left and now even she was ready to jump ship and leave Jillian to fend for herself.

Flashbacks from the week began zipping through Brianna's head like an instant video replay.

How Monday night at the swim meet, instead of congratulating Mimi on her third-place ribbon for the freestyle heat, Jillian had to show off her blue ribbon for the 50-meter butterfly.

And how on Tuesday at gymnastics, Jillian just had to tell all the Level 5s about the five ribbons she had won at the Level 6 competition on Saturday. She never even asked how the Level 5s had done on Sunday at their tournament.

Nothing too terrible came to mind for Wednesday, but Thursday and Friday came through loud and clear.

Thursday Jillian just had to tell Haley what she was going to wear to Brandon's party even though she knew Haley hadn't been invited.

And now Friday morning had been absolutely the last straw! Everything from that morning came back to Brianna in living color. They had just finished band practice and, as they were putting away their instruments, Mr. Paulsen read off the names of the kids who would be doing the solos for the spring musical.

When he read off Brianna's name for the flute solo, everyone crowded around her, congratulating her and high-fiving her. Everyone except Jillian. Jillian was nowhere to be seen.

Brianna knew that Jillian would be disappointed that she didn't get the flute solo, but she didn't expect Jillian to come all unhinged the way she had.

At noon Jillian had called Brianna "a traitor" and was no longer even speaking to her.

The more Brianna thought about Jillian, the more upset she got, and she could feel her stomach twisting into an angry knot.

She finally decided that if Jillian didn't want to be friends anymore, that was okay with her. Or was it?

Brianna and Jillian had been friends for a lot of years. It was Jillian who persuaded Brianna to try out for the spring operetta in third grade. And Brianna had been in every operetta since then.

And it was Jillian who taught her how to ice-skate when everyone else had given up on her. Brianna remembered how patient Jillian had been back then.

Brianna was as fed up with Jillian as anyone, but she felt someone should talk to her and tell her why she was losing all her friends. That was the only fair thing to do.

But who would talk to her? She didn't feel it was her job to do it. But if she didn't, who would?

If you were Brianna, what would *you* do? Why?

More to think about:

Do you think Jillian is a "good sport"? Why or why not?

Why do you think it's important for her always to be "#1"?

Do you know someone like Jillian?

What might happen to Jillian if Brianna drops her too?

Do you think a real friend would talk to Jillian? Why or why not?

Egg Rolls, Tortillas, and Collard Greens

"So what's a 'block party' anyway?" Spencer asked, plunking his lunch tray down on the table and sliding onto the bench next to Nathan.

Nathan blew a giant bubble with his gum and then inhaled the bubble slowly with a long hissing sound. "Our neighborhood has a block party every summer in the park with a pig roast and all the trimmings. We all bring food and games and we have a blast. And now that you've moved into our neighborhood, you're included, too."

"Last year our team won the softball game," Jasmine pointed out. "And we're going to do it again this year."

"Yeah, right!" Nathan grunted. "Mitchell will be pitching this year and that means your team will be lucky if you score even one run."

"So what's so great about a block party anyway?" Spencer asked, carefully picking the olives off his pizza.

Jasmine squeezed her eyes shut and smiled. "Just wait till you see all the food. Picture tables and tables of incredible goodies. Mrs. Yue and her

family always bring zillions of her special egg rolls. She spends days in her kitchen just getting ready for the block party. And Mrs. Sanchez brings her own fabulous tortillas made from a recipe that goes back generations."

"And Kathleen Kelly and her family bring a ton of pasta. Real home-made pasta like you've never tasted in your whole entire life," Selena added, licking her lips. "The tomato sauce is loaded with mushrooms and sausage and red and green peppers and a ton of garlic. Everyone always wants to know the recipe, but Mrs. Kelly will never tell anyone because she says it's a family secret."

"And don't forget my mom and all her soul food," Gregory interrupted, grinning. "Man, you ain't tasted nothin' till you've inhaled some of my mama's chitlins, ham hocks, and collard greens."

Spencer stuck his finger down his throat and pretended to gag. "What on earth are 'chitlins'?"

Selena shook her head and rolled her eyes. "Trust me, you don't want to know. Just eat and enjoy and don't ask any questions. Sometimes it's better not to know what you're eating!"

Nathan nodded. "Gregory's right. His mom's soul food is really great, but so is everything there."

Spencer shoveled a piece of pizza into his mouth and frowned. "So what about those new apartments across from us? You know, where all those people on welfare live? Do we invite them?"

Jasmine shrugged. "It's called 'subsidized housing' because they don't pay as much rent as most people do. That's where Letitia and Vernon live and I'm going to ask Letitia to be on our softball team this year. She is one great hitter!"

Spencer's frown grew even bigger. "But the people in those apartments aren't like us. I hear that a lot of them get food stamps and some of them don't even have jobs. Do we have to invite them to the block party?"

Gregory gave Spencer a hefty whack on the back. "Hey, man, what do you know anyway? Have you ever been on welfare? I have and it's no picnic. The people in those apartments are no different from us."

Jasmine dug through her backpack and pulled out a crumpled paper. "This is the flyer from last year. My mom prints up the flyers on her computer and then we all deliver them to the houses and churches near us. We even post some of the flyers on the bulletin boards at local stores. We figure the more people who come the better."

Nathan chugalugged the rest of his milk and eyeballed Spencer. "So what do you say? Do you want to help us deliver the flyers to the apartments or not?"

If you were Spencer, what would *you* do? Why?

More to think about:

Do you think the people in the apartments want to be invited?

Do you think the kids in the apartments are really that different from Nathan and his friends? Why or why not?

How do you think the people in the apartments will feel if they aren't invited?

What do you think determines a person's "worth"? How much money she or he has? What kind of job he or she has?

Do you only choose friends who are just like you? Why or why not?

The Jackson Four

"So what do I do now?" Mario groaned, as he tossed his empty lunch bag into the trash bin next to the soccer field.

Nicole rolled her eyes and shook her head. "They did it to you again, right?"

Mario nodded. "Right! They took my lunch and tossed me the empty lunch bag. I'm just no match for Kyle and Derek."

Then Elyssa let loose with a groan, too. "Tell me about it. Derek grabbed my homework for Spanish class right out of my Spanish book and I had nothing to turn in to Ms. Garcia. Mario's right. We're no match for the Gruesome Twosome."

Lee nodded. "I know what you mean. They're always calling me 'Chink' or 'Slant-Eyes' and last week I heard them calling Jasmine 'Blubber Lips.'"

Nicole made a "T" with her two index fingers and signaled a time-out. "Guys, why do we call ourselves the 'Jackson Four'?"

Elyssa fixed her dark brown eyes on Nicole like lasers. "Girl, you know why. Because we all live on Jackson Street."

Nicole flashed her a thumbs-up. "And what is our motto?"

"One for all and all for one," Mario and Lee chorused together. "You know that."

Nicole gave a low whistle. "I know that *I* know it, but it seems that the three of you have forgotten it. What that means is that if one of us has a problem, *all* of us have a problem."

Elyssa crossed her eyes and groaned again. "Okay, so now all four of us have a problem. How does that help any of us?"

Nicole stopped smiling and eyeballed the group. "I think what we have here is a serious attitude problem. Let's try looking at this situation as a challenge."

"Yeah, right. A challenge to die for," Mario added, as he drew a finger across his throat.

Elyssa opened her bag of chips and popped one into her mouth. "Okay, girl, I'm listening. Just where are you going with this 'challenge' thing? And where do we start?"

Nicole slipped her backpack off her shoulders and sat down on the grass. "We start by using our heads, not our muscles. And I think we'll start with Mario's lunch. If Kyle wants Mario's sandwich so badly, I say we give it to him."

Elyssa almost choked on a chip. "What? I thought the whole idea here was to get these guys off our backs, not surrender!"

"Right, and that's exactly what we're going to do," Nicole said, closing her eyes and smiling. "I see a very special peanut butter sandwich in Kyle's future. Peanut butter with a little horseradish, a few *very* hot chili peppers, some sauerkraut, and mucho garlic. I will personally make Mario's lunch tomorrow, and I promise it will be a lunch to remember."

Lee stopped cracking his knuckles and grinned. "You know, this reminds me of a story my father likes to tell. It seems this man had three sons who were always arguing and couldn't work together, so the father has each of them break one stick which he has removed from an old broomstick. Then the father hands each of them the broom and tells them to try breaking the sticks that are bound together. Of course, they can't do it and he tells them that when they stand alone, they are weak, but like the broomstick, working together brings strength."

Nicole shot Lee a thumbs-up. "I think you've just given me an answer to the riddle Ms. Porter gave our social studies class. She wants us to give her an example on Monday of how the whole can be greater than the sum of its parts and I've got the perfect example. It's us! All four of us!

"Just think about it for a minute. The four of us working together as a team are greater than any one of us working alone. Together we can succeed where alone we each might have given up.

"So what do you say, Mario? Do you want me to make my very special, never-to-be-forgotten peanut butter sandwich for your lunch tomorrow?"

If you were Mario, what would *you* do? Why?

Why do you think some kids pick on other kids?

Are there any bullies at your school?

How do you handle them?

What do you think of Nicole's idea of working together?

Do you have any other ideas for Nicole and her friends?

The Troublesome Triangle

Kara scribbled over the twos on the cover of her notebook and began drawing threes. Then she blacked out the threes and drew a zero. A big fat zero.

One big fat zero for her life. Her life had gone from a happy two to a dismal zero in less than a month, thanks to Melissa.

It had always been just the two of them, Kara and Ashley. They had been best friends since the third grade and they had sworn they would be best friends forever.

They even liked the same kind of pizza—double cheese—and they both hated broccoli and peanut butter.

Then Melissa moved into the neighborhood and everything changed. It was like that nursery rhyme about Mary and her little lamb. Only in this case, it was everywhere that Ashley went, Melissa was sure to follow.

It seemed that Ashley couldn't do anything anymore without including Melissa. And it didn't take a rocket scientist to see that Ashley and

Melissa were spending more and more time together and that Kara was the one who was left out.

It wasn't that Ashley and Melissa didn't try to include her, because they did. Last week they asked her to go to the movies with them on Saturday. But there was no way Kara would go anywhere or do anything with Melissa, so she told them she already had other plans.

Now Ashley and Melissa were busy planning a big Halloween party and they had asked Kara to help them.

Again, Kara told them no. She had hoped that if she kept refusing to do anything with Melissa, eventually Ashley would come to her senses and dump her.

But so far things weren't working out that way. Ashley and Melissa were spending more time with each other, while Kara was spending more time alone in her room.

Kara tried talking to her mother about the problem, but her mother just didn't understand. Her response had been simply, "Why can't all three of you be friends? Aren't two friends better than one anyway?" So much for her mother's help.

Then she tried talking to her dad and he hadn't been much better. He suggested that she invite both girls over for an overnight with pizza.

Yeah, right! Invite the enemy over for pizza. That sure made a lot of sense.

All she wanted was her best friend back and things the way they used to be. Was that asking too much?

At dinner that night while her dad talked about plans for their summer vacation, all Kara could think about was how to eliminate Melissa from her life.

She stared at the crackers floating on top of her tomato soup. She hated tomato soup. Tomato soup always reminded her of how she had thrown up all over the lunch table in the third grade and how Ashley had gone with her to the nurse's office.

That's how it had always been. A straight line between two dots: just she and Ashley. Now the straight line had been taken over by a triangle and Kara wanted no part of it.

She knew that if she kept turning down their invitations to do things, pretty soon Ashley and Melissa might just stop asking her. And then it would be a straight line again: just Ashley and Melissa.

She was still thinking about straight lines and triangles when the telephone rang. It was Ashley, asking again if Kara wanted to help them plan the Halloween party.

She was about to say no and give Ashley some phony excuse, but then she stopped herself. What if this was the last time Ashley ever asked her to do anything with them? She might just have a lot to lose here!

If you were Kara, what would *you* do? Why?

More to think about:

Why do you think Kara doesn't want to be Melissa's friend?

How do you think Melissa is feeling?

What might happen if Kara keeps saying no to Ashley and Melissa?

Can you have two best friends at the same time? Why or why not?

Do you think it's okay for Kara to treat Ashley and Melissa the way she is treating them? Why or why not?

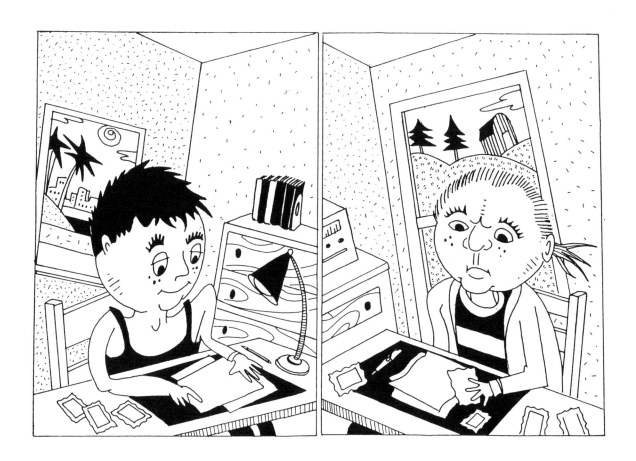

Mirror, Mirror, on the Wall

In the beginning Casey had thought it was a great idea and she had been one of the first to sign up!

Ms. Porter always came up with cool ideas for her social studies class. This time she had come up with the idea of writing to kids in a school clear across the country. And California was about as far away from Pennsylvania as you could get.

Ms. Porter had a teacher friend who taught fifth grade at a Los Angeles school and her class thought it would be fun to write to kids in a fifth-grade class at a different school in a different state.

Everyone in Casey's class drew names out of a hat and Casey drew Bradley's name. That was two months ago and writing to Bradley had been a lot of fun.

She brought her letter to class every Friday and then Ms. Porter mailed it with all the other letters in a huge envelope.

Casey had learned a lot about Bradley. He loved soccer and football and hated baseball. He loved hot dogs, hamburgers, and pizza, and he hated veggies and applesauce.

And she had even discovered that they liked a lot of the same things—like horror films and sci-fi books.

But then last week Bradley had sent her a picture of himself and asked her to send him one of her.

Bradley's picture was just how she had pictured him. Red hair, freckles, and, of course, he was holding a soccer ball.

But there was no way she could send him a picture of herself. The braces were bad enough, but her body was a real disaster.

Her dad called her "pleasingly plump," but the bathroom scale told a different story. She was fifteen pounds overweight according to the chart in her doctor's office. Doc Turner always told her that she was just at the top end of the normal range for her age and there was no reason to worry. Easy for *him* to say!

She pulled out all her photo albums and leafed through them page by page, but it looked hopeless. She automatically rejected any photo of her smiling because of the braces.

The only possibility was a photo of her on a horse at camp last summer. The horse took up most of the picture and you couldn't really see what the rider looked like.

She finally gave up on the photo albums. Soon she found herself in the bathroom studying her reflection in the mirror. There was no way she could send Bradley a picture of herself. One look at her picture and he would never write another letter.

She felt desperate and all kinds of ideas began whirling around in her head. She could send a picture of her sister Molly, who had tons of pictures lying around. She'd never even miss one. And Molly was definitely cute. And skinny.

But in her heart of hearts she knew she couldn't really send Molly's picture. That would be like telling a lie. A big lie.

What if she just ignored Bradley's request and didn't send any picture? That seemed like a promising solution, at least for now.

But how long could she do that? Wouldn't Bradley begin to wonder why she didn't send a picture? Somewhere down the line she would have to come up with some believable excuse.

Casey glanced again at the brown eyes in the mirror. The brown eyes were good. They were her best feature. Maybe she could just cut the head off one of her pictures with her mouth closed and send that.

Yeah, right! Then he really would wonder what was going on if he received a picture of just her head.

Tomorrow was Friday, so she didn't have much time left to decide.

If you were Casey, what would *you* do? Why?

More to think about:

Why do you think Casey is so hung up about her weight?

How important is honesty? Do you think Casey should just send Bradley a picture? Why or why not?

What would you think about Bradley if he sees Casey's picture and is no longer interested in being her friend?

How important is physical appearance to you?

What advice would you give Casey if she were your friend? Why?

Black Thursday

My name's Eliot and my problem began last Thursday. That's why I call it Black Thursday. That's when Ms. Bradshaw, our language arts teacher, told our class that we had to finish up our book reports by Monday and be ready to give our oral book reports.

The good news is that we could choose any book. The bad news is that I don't read books.

Why should I read books when I can learn just as much from watching TV? And why should I worry about learning how to write when I can talk? If we're talking about real communication here, anyone knows that you can say a lot more and in much less time by talking than by writing.

There are a lot of things I *do* like about school—like recess and lunch and gym class and field trips and a whole bunch of other things. I just don't like to read books or write papers.

And I especially don't like to give speeches. It's not that I'm all that shy, I just don't like having to stand up there in front of the whole class and talk.

My heart starts pounding double-time, my hands get all sweaty, and my mouth is so dry that I can hardly talk.

Anyway, Ms. Bradshaw assigned us to teams, with three kids to a team. Both the kids on my team are really smart. They both read the book in one night. It took me three days to get through it.

Aaron can really draw, so he did all the pictures for the book report. And Katie is a computer whiz, so she offered to type our report for us.

That left me to do the oral report! All weekend I thought about nothing else. Videos kept running through my head: twenty million different ways how I could mess up and look like a real dork!

I was hoping that by Monday I could come down with some kind of weird illness that would keep me home. But no such luck!

Monday came and I didn't even have the sniffles. So that's why I'm sitting here in my math class counting the dots on the girl's shirt in front of me.

While Mr. Marcus is talking about fractions, I'm still trying to think of ways to get out of doing the oral book report.

It's bad enough looking like a dork on my own, but this time I'm part of a team and the grades for our report will depend on *all* of us. What a bummer!

As I head to my next class, I feel like I'm walking down Death Row to my execution.

I'm taking a last drink at the water fountain before going into class when Russell punches me hard in the arm.

"Hey, Eliot, are you ready for Ms. Bradshaw's class? Man, you don't look too good! You're whiter than these walls here."

I'm thinking that Russell is right. I probably look as lousy as I feel, so why not head upstairs to the nurse's office? It would be easy to fake a stomach ache. Or maybe I could actually throw up.

But if I chicken out today, that just means I'll have to give the report tomorrow, and that really doesn't solve my problem.

So what do I do? Fake a natural disaster or bite the bullet and get the report over with? There's something to be said for getting it over with, even if it means looking like a dork and letting my team down.

Meanwhile, Russell's staring at me like he's waiting for me to make up my mind. Do I go into class with him or take the easy way out and head for the nurse's office?

If you were Eliot, what would *you* do? Why?

More to think about:

Have you ever felt the way Eliot feels?

Why do you think it's so hard for him to give an oral report to his class?

If he doesn't face his problem now, do you think the problem will "go away"? Why or why not?

Do you think it takes courage to deal with a problem like this?

What advice would you give Eliot?

No Perfect 10

Only Clayton could strike out three times in a row and still smile. No wonder all the guys called him a dork.

I sneaked a quick peek at the bleachers. Eddie was doing his finger-across-the-throat thing and Jamal was covering his eyes like he couldn't stand to watch any more of the game.

Instead of going back to the dugout and sitting with the guys after he struck out, Clayton began picking up empty pop cans and tossing them in the recycling bin. He's always doing stuff like that. It's like he thinks he's on a personal mission to save the earth.

And when the guys are talking about football and soccer, good old Clayton is spouting off facts about how fossil fuels can cause global warming. Clayton is seriously uncool.

As usual, our team, the Wildcats, lost and I watched Clayton head home, still picking up litter and stuffing it in his pockets.

As I headed to the locker room, I had no idea that my world as I knew it was about to crash and burn.

My friends were already there waiting for me. Anthony was laughing so hard, he was just about doubled over, holding his stomach.

"So is this a great idea or is this a great idea?" he finally managed to sputter, while he leaned against his locker to keep from falling over.

Eddie slapped him on the back and grinned. "You're a genius, man. Maybe not in math, but this is a seriously brilliant idea."

Jamal gave him a thumbs-up. "Totally cool, bro."

If it was Anthony's idea, I knew someone was going to get hurt and all my sensors were sounding a red alert. But I asked anyway. "So what's going on?"

Since Anthony was off on another laughing binge, Eddie tried to explain.

"You know how Clayton invited the four of us to his birthday party next Saturday?"

Then Jamal screwed up his face and mimicked Clayton's scratchy voice. "'Do you think that maybe if you're not doing anything else you might be able to come over to my house on Saturday to help me celebrate my birthday? That is, if you're not already doing something else?'"

Then Eddie took over again. "So Anthony comes up with this really brilliant idea. We're all going to tell Clayton we're coming to his party and then none of us are going to show up. Let's roll the video: I can see Clayton now. He's pacing back and forth wondering where everyone is. It's getting later and later and still no one shows up."

While Eddie was rolling his imaginary video, Anthony grabbed his throat with both hands. Then he stuck out his tongue and looked cross-eyed. "And then maybe he'll finally get it. We don't want to be his friends. So, when are we going to be his friends? Never! That's when. When are we going to be his friends?"

The other guys echoed, "Never, that's when!"

I could feel my face heating up and my stomach twisting into a knot. Clayton would probably never be my best friend, but I sure didn't want to be responsible for him self-destructing either.

I knew that what Anthony and the guys were going to do was wrong, but I felt helpless.

Eddie pounded me on the back and shot me a grin. "So, Travis, are you with us?"

If you were Travis, what would *you* do? Why?

More to think about:

Do you think it's okay to do what Anthony and his friend are planning to do? Why or why not?

How do you think Clayton will feel if the boys don't show up at his party?

Do you know someone like Clayton?

How do the other kids treat him or her?

How do you treat him or her?

How do you think Travis will feel if he goes along with Anthony's plan? Why?

Show-and-Don't-Tell

The threat was still ringing in Ken's ears as he biked home from school. "Listen, kid, you tell anyone what you saw, and you'll be sorry you ever came to this school."

Talk about being in the wrong place at the wrong time! He had been using one of the stalls in the boys' bathroom that morning and when he came out to wash his hands, there was a group of older boys huddled in the corner.

One of the guys had brought a gun from home to show his friends and each of the boys was taking a turn holding the gun and pretending to aim at an imaginary target.

That's when Robb aimed the gun right at Ken and gave him the warning. Ken had never been that close to a real gun before in his whole life and he could feel his heart pounding inside his chest as Robb aimed the gun at him and smiled this really weird smile.

Robb had a reputation for being a bully. He was the biggest kid in the

entire sixth grade, and the only thing bigger than his body was his bad attitude. He was always picking on someone. Always someone smaller and younger.

Robb's warning was enough for Ken! He didn't even stick around long enough to see if there were any bullets in the gun. He got out of there as fast as he could and headed to the cafeteria for lunch.

While he was standing in the lunch line, two of Robb's friends from the restroom pushed their way into the line behind him. They didn't say anything, but their message came through loud and clear.

If Ken said anything to anyone, he would have *them* to answer to.

He thought about nothing else the rest of the day. In math class while Mr. Marcus was talking about percentages, Ken was thinking about threats. Ken didn't doubt for a minute that Robb or one of his friends would make good on their threat.

And during his science lab while Ms. Jacobs was talking about cloud formations, Ken was thinking about other formations: Robb and his gang. He planned to stay as far away from them as he could for the rest of the school year.

Biking home, he told himself the only smart thing to do was to keep his mouth shut and not tell anyone about the gun. It wasn't like the guys were really going to do anything with it. He was pretty sure they were just showing off and horsing around.

Then he remembered how Nick had been threatening to get even with Mr. Grant, the basketball coach, for kicking him off the team.

Nick was one of Robb's friends and, at the time, Ken hadn't even taken the threat seriously. But that was before he had seen the gun. Now he didn't know what to think.

Should he tell Coach Grant about Nick's threats? Maybe he didn't even know how angry Nick was. Ken liked Coach Grant a lot, but what if he told the coach about Nick's threats and Robb and his friends found out?

There was always Mr. Evans, the school counselor. Ken knew that school counselors were supposed to keep whatever you said to them "confidential" and not tell anyone else. But was telling a school counselor almost the same as telling the police?

He also knew he could talk it over with his older brother Jake. He could talk to Jake about almost anything, and talking to his brother wouldn't really be like "squealing" since Jake was still a kid himself.

By the time Ken reached his garage and had put his bike away, he was more confused than ever. He still wasn't sure what he should do.

If you were Ken, what would *you* do? Why?

More to think about:

What might happen if Ken doesn't tell anyone about the gun?

How do you think he will feel if he doesn't tell anyone about the gun and someone gets hurt?

Do you think Ken should tell Coach Grant about the threat? Why or why not?

What advice do you think his brother Jake would give him?

What advice would you give Ken? Why?

Blindfolds and Bugles

It all started with Eric. It was the first day of school and Ms. Benjamin asked me, Matthew Christopher Morgan, to be Eric's buddy for the first week. She wanted me to show him around and eat lunch with him till he made some friends of his own.

Now I've got to tell you right up front that I held my breath and slumped down in my seat as far as I could, so Ms. B. wouldn't see me, but she beamed every table with those huge brown eyes of hers and then stopped right at my table. And then right on me.

It's not so much that I minded being Eric's babysitter because he was new. It was more because he was deaf. Like really deaf. He has a lady who signs for him in some of his classes, and I've heard the other kids laugh when Eric messes up.

Well, after a week of hanging out with Eric, I've got to tell you, I learned a whole lot I never knew before. Like deaf kids are really just like us regular kids. They like football and baseball and they even chew bubble gum and hate spinach.

But I still wasn't sure I wanted to invite him to my birthday party. I was pretty sure the other guys would give me a hard time if I did because Eric is just "different" from the rest of us.

That first week with Eric also got me thinking about all the stuff I take for granted since my own ears work pretty well. Like the sounds of guitars strumming and frogs croaking and balloons popping and dogs barking. And if I were deaf, would I still be able to play my bugle? I don't think so!

Well, I guess this thing with Eric got Ms. Benjamin thinking too because the day before our Thanksgiving vacation, she gave everyone in our class a number.

We thought maybe we were going to play some really cool game or something, but then she handed out blindfolds to all the kids with odd numbers. I had a pretty good idea what was coming next.

You guessed it. I was number 11, so I got a blindfold. Then she told us to put the blindfolds on because we were going to experience what it's like to be blind all morning.

The kids with even numbers were our partners and they had to stick to us like glue to make sure we didn't get into any serious trouble—like walking into a brick wall or anything.

Since Eric was number 12, he was my partner. As I tied my blindfold on, I felt goose bumps break out all over my body. What if I did something really dumb, like accidentally sit down on somebody's lap or something?

The first thirty minutes were a piece of cake. We all just sat there listening to Mrs. Preston, the office secretary, read off all the news bulletins and messages over the public address system.

But then it was time for current events and things began to get a little hairy. It was my table's turn to share news that we read about in the newspaper, and I could feel my stomach doing flipflops. I didn't like feeling different from the other kids.

Jeffrey talked for a few minutes about the ozone layer and then it was my turn.

Eric had hold of my elbow and he kind of propelled me forward. I didn't like that helpless feeling at all and I felt my face beginning to get hotter when I heard some laughs at some of the other tables. Only this time they were laughing at me. It didn't feel very good.

I talked for a few minutes about the problems in the Middle East, but it felt like hours. I felt like a goldfish in a bowl with everyone staring at me. I wished that I had known what Ms. Benjamin was planning, so I could have called in sick.

To tell you the truth, I was beginning to feel pretty sick for real. My stomach was churning up a storm and it felt like I had a golf ball stuck in my throat.

And I was thinking about Eric. Did I want to change my mind about not inviting him to my birthday party?

If you were Matthew, what would *you* do? Why?

More to think about:

How do you think Eric feels when the other kids laugh at him?

Why do you think the other kids are ignoring him?

What do you think Matthew has learned from hanging out with Eric?

Why do you think Ms. Benjamin did her little experiment?

Do you think the other kids learned anything from Ms. Benjamin's experiment?

Round and Round I Go . . .

It all started with a lie. It wasn't even a big lie, as lies go.

My name's Anna, and if you have a few minutes, I'll tell you all the gory details.

On Tuesday I told Kathy I'd go bowling with her on Saturday. And on Tuesday, I really did want to go bowling.

But that was before Wednesday came and Leslie invited me to go with her to a baseball game on Saturday. Now I've got to tell you, I really love baseball, so I knew what I had to do.

I called Kathy and told her I had to baby-sit my little brother, Mikey, so I couldn't go bowling after all.

I could tell she felt really bad, but what could I do? I could go bowling any time, but how often did I get a chance to see a professional baseball game up close and for real instead of watching one on TV?

I didn't like to lie and I knew it wasn't right, but what choice did I have? I really wanted to go to that game.

That is, I really wanted to see the game until Thursday night when Allison called and invited me to go up to her cabin at the lake for the whole weekend with her family.

Now bowling was a lot of fun and a real live baseball game was great, but I had never been to Allison's cabin. What if I said no and she never invited me again? So what could I do? I sure didn't want to miss out on a whole weekend at the lake.

So I told Allison yes and then I called Leslie and told her I couldn't go to the game after all because my grandmother was coming to visit us and I had to stay home to spend time with her.

So far, so good. It looked like everyone believed me. Kathy told me she was sorry I couldn't go bowling, but maybe we could go the next weekend. And Leslie told me she was sorry I couldn't go to the game, but there would be other games.

So far I was scoring 2 for 2. Two little lies didn't seem too bad, considering that now I was going to have a whole glorious weekend up at the lake.

I didn't like lying to my friends, but what could I do? I didn't want to miss out on a weekend at the lake.

But then Friday afternoon my whole world came crashing down around me. Allison called to let me know her mom had the flu and they wouldn't be going to the lake after all.

But that was okay. I knew there was still Leslie and the baseball game. So I called Leslie and let the phone ring, but all I got was a message telling me that the Ryans would not be available until Sunday.

Bummer! So I called Kathy, hoping that we could still go bowling.

77

I had to try to remember which lie I had told her, but I was pretty sure it was the one about having to baby-sit my brother.

Kathy's mom answered the phone, but it was just more bad news. She told me that Kathy was spending the night at Tanya's and that they were going bowling from Tanya's house on Saturday.

Not fair! It looked like my weekend had gone from incredibly great to a national disaster in a matter of minutes.

This was going to be a very long weekend without my friends.

Lying to your friends could really mess up your life a lot and I asked myself what I would do if I could do an instant replay of last week and do things differently.

If you were Anna and you could go back to Tuesday, what would *you* do? What would you tell Kathy, Leslie, and Allison? Why?

More to think about:

Do you think it's okay for Anna to treat her friends the way she is treating them? Why or why not?

Do you think she is treating them fairly and with the respect they deserve?

Would you want a friend like Anna? Why or why not?

If she had gone to the lake with Allison, do you think Kathy and Leslie might have found out?

What do you think Anna has learned from all this?

So Who's Counting?

Rachel had been looking forward to this day all year! She loved track almost as much as she loved basketball, and this was the final track meet of the season.

She had done even better than she had hoped and she felt ten feet high as she looped her winning ribbons through the zipper of her gym bag,

She would remember this day for the rest of her life! She had tied for first place in the hundred-yard dash and come in second in the broad jump. Then in her last event, the four-forty, she came in first just ahead of Natalie who had tied with her in the hundred-yard dash.

She might never have another day like this ever again, she told herself as she pulled on her warm-up jacket and jogged on over to the pop stand to celebrate her victories with her friends.

That's when she saw it! The huge sign that said no contestant could enter more than two events or they would be disqualified from the meet.

Since she had arrived late, she had missed the usual warm-up session

with Coach Emerson. That's when they always reviewed any special rules for the day.

Now that she knew about the rule and realized that she had been illegally entered in her third event, she didn't know what to do.

The easiest thing would be to do nothing. No one seemed to have noticed that she had been in more than two events, not even Coach Emerson.

And it would sure be embarrassing to have to return her third ribbon to the track judges and try to explain everything.

Then she read the sign again. It said she would be "disqualified" if she entered more than two events. Would that mean she would have to return *all* her ribbons?

She couldn't believe it. Her day had just gone from superterrific to horribly dismal in less than five minutes.

She knew what her friends would tell her to do. They would tell her to keep quiet and "not cause waves." Like the time the cashier at the mall gave her back too much money and she wanted to go back and return it.

Lisa had told her to cool her jets and not be such a "worry wart," and Ariana had echoed Lisa's message loud and clear. She told her to "loosen up."

In the end, she had listened to her friends and not returned the money, but she had never felt right about it. But that was old news. Now she had a new problem to deal with!

Maybe she could find Coach Emerson and ask her what to do, but would she just get mad at her? Mad because Rachel had been late and missed their warm-up session and mad because she had messed up big-time and created a problem for everyone.

The meet was just winding down, so she didn't have much time left to decide.

Should she try to explain to the judges and probably have everyone in the whole school talking about her for the next month?

Or should she just play it cool and not say anything? But what if the judges realized the error later? What would they think? And what would they do?

Rachel knew she was stuck between a rock and a hard place. She could feel the sweat trickling down the back of her neck, but she knew it was now or never. She had to make a decision.

If you were Rachel, what would *you* do? Why?

More to think about:

How do you think Rachel will feel every time she looks at her ribbons if she doesn't say anything?

Do you think Coach Emerson will be angry if Rachel explains the problem to her? Why or why not?

How do you think Natalie will feel if she finds out?

What do you think the judges will think if they find out?

If you were Rachel's friend, what would you tell her to do? Why?

Unfair Penalty

All the kids in Todd's neighborhood had been invited to Antonio's pool party on Saturday. All the kids, that is, except one. Leon.

Antonio told Todd that he wanted to invite Leon, but both his parents said no! They told him that Leon might be a "bad influence" on all the other kids.

Todd knew that Leon's family had problems. Plenty of problems. Last year his older brother had been caught breaking into someone's house and just last month his younger sister was picked up for shoplifting. And Todd knew that Leon's mom worked two jobs so the family wouldn't have to go on welfare.

Todd also knew that Leon himself had a clean slate. He had never experimented with drugs, and he was always on his mother's case to try to get her to quit her pack-a-day cigarette habit.

It didn't seem fair that Leon should be penalized for something that wasn't his fault. He didn't know if Leon even knew about the party, but what if he found out about it?

And what if Leon asked Todd to go bowling or something on Saturday? Last Saturday Todd had gone hiking with Leon's scout troop and had a great time.

What if Leon asked him to do something this Saturday? What does he say? Does he tell Leon the truth? Does he make up some phony excuse? And what if Leon learns the truth later?

On Wednesday Todd checked again with Antonio to see if Antonio's parents had changed their mind about Leon. But Antonio just shrugged and told him that his parents were really "dug in" on the subject of Leon and were not about to change their minds.

On Thursday Todd checked with some of the other guys to see if they were going to Antonio's party. They all agreed that it was too bad Leon hadn't been invited, but there was nothing they could do about it. And everyone was still planning to go to Antonio's on Saturday. After all, it was Leon's problem, not theirs.

Saturday was approaching fast and Todd still didn't know what he was going to do.

He thought about asking his dad to speak to Antonio's dad and try to explain how Leon was on the honor roll and not into drugs or anything else. He wasn't sure his dad would feel comfortable doing that, but he knew he could always ask him.

He even thought about talking to Antonio's mom and dad himself and asking them to reconsider. He could remind them how hard Leon had worked mowing lawns last summer to earn money for soccer camp. But talking to someone else's parents would be pretty tough. Especially about something that really wasn't any of his business. They certainly had a right to invite whoever they wanted to Antonio's party.

Todd was beginning to feel brain dead from thinking so much and he was fresh out of new ideas.

He really wanted to go to Antonio's party, but it would be hard to have a good time if he wasn't sure he was doing the right thing.

Todd's dad was always telling him to "weigh the consequences" when he had a tough decision to make. So what were the consequences here? It looked like a lose-lose situation.

If Todd goes to the party, he knows he'll probably be thinking about Leon the whole time.

But if he doesn't go to the party, will he be sorry that he missed out on a good time with all his friends?

The more Todd thought about the problem, the more confused he got. Should he go or not? Maybe the guys were right, that it was Leon's problem, not his.

If you were Todd, what would *you* do? Why?

More to think about:

Do you think Leon knows about the party?

If he does know, how do you think he feels?

Can you understand how Antonio's parents feel?

Do you think Antonio's parents know all the facts?

Do you think this is only Leon's problem? Why or why not?

The Intimidating Initiation

Megan stared at the note in her hand and reread the words for the zillionth time.

DON'T MISS THIS SCAVENGER HUNT! IT'S THE CHANCE OF A LIFETIME!

The words were true enough. This might be her only chance to ever join the COOL GIRLS CLUB.

The girls in the COOL GIRLS CLUB were just that. Very, very cool! They wore the coolest clothes, they had the coolest parties, and they only associated with other cool girls.

The note in her hand looked innocent enough. Find a gold watch, a red T-shirt, and a purple bathing suit.

But Megan knew what the initiation was really all about. If you wanted to join the COOL GIRLS CLUB, you had to shoplift everything on the list and a club member would shadow you to be sure you did just that.

Kayla Martin was assigned to be her shadow. Kayla was just about the most popular girl in the whole sixth grade and any kid would give a week's allowance to be invited to one of her parties.

She knew Kayla would be watching her like a hawk to be sure she really did shoplift all three items on the list.

Megan knew shoplifting was wrong, but when she pictured those purple windbreakers with the words "COOL GIRLS CLUB" printed on the back, she knew she just had to have one. To have one of those jackets would be a dream come true.

Next Friday was D-Day. Decision Day. And Megan had no idea what she was going to do. Would she actually have the nerve to show up and steal everything on the list?

On Monday she told herself YES! After all, what was the big deal anyway? All three things on the list probably came to less than fifty dollars and it wasn't like the store was going to go broke or anything.

On Tuesday, she wasn't quite so sure. She reminded herself that shoplifting was really stealing. And, anyway you looked at it, stealing was wrong.

By Wednesday she wasn't sure she could do it and was having serious second thoughts. She was beginning to change her mind about even showing up on Friday.

But on Thursday she had lunch with Kayla and Kayla let her try on her COOL GIRLS CLUB jacket. It was like magic. Wearing that jacket made her feel incredible. Like Cinderella, Snow White, and Princess Di all rolled into one.

By Friday it felt like butterflies were doing somersaults in her stomach. Or maybe something bigger like bats. But she told herself that she just couldn't miss out on this once-in-a-lifetime opportunity and decided to go for it.

She got to the mall at five o'clock, hoping that maybe Kayla wouldn't even show up and that the whole thing had just been one big joke. Maybe a test that she would pass just by showing up.

But Kayla was already there waiting for her, grinning from ear to ear.

Kayla slapped her a high-five. "Way to go, girl. I knew you'd show up. Just think, an hour from now you'll be one of us. Do you have your list?"

Megan nodded. "Right here. Let's just get it over with before I lose my nerve."

Kayla slapped her another high-five and and dropped back a few feet while she looked at some rings at the jewelry counter.

Megan stopped at the display of watches on a table in the center aisle and picked up one of the gift boxes. She opened the lid and carefully took the watch out.

The delicate gold band was so elegant. She felt her palms beginning to sweat and she could feel her whole body covered in goose bumps. But it was now or never.

If you were Megan, what would *you* do? Why?

More to think about:

Megan knows that shoplifting is wrong but she's seriously thinking about doing it anyway. Why?

How do you think she will feel if she does shoplift?

What could happen to her if she gets caught shoplifting?

Is shoplifting really stealing when it's for a club initiation?

What do you think about the COOL GIRLS CLUB and their initiation?

Is this a club you would want to join? Why or why not?

Henry Harrison and the Horribly Hairy Hot Dog

My name is Jeremy Sullivan and I should have known better. When Henry Harrison offered to trade me his hot dog for my peanut butter and pickle sandwich, my sensors should have sounded a red alert. But they didn't, so I did. I traded.

I shot a glob of mustard on the dog and then took a big bite. That's when I knew he had done it to me again!

I spit what was in my mouth onto my plate and looked down at it. There in the mess was a hairy spider looking up at me and I thought I was going to barf right on the spot.

Meanwhile Henry was laughing so hard, he was about falling off his chair. So then I took a closer look and realized the hairy thing looking up at me was one of Henry's fake spiders.

He's got a whole bunch of fake stuff: fake spiders, fake throw-up, and even fake dog doo-doo.

I knew I had to even the score. But how? No one in our whole class had ever put one over on Henry Harrison.

And then it came to me right out of the blue. I knew exactly what I would do. It would be a piece of cake and Henry would finally get what he deserved. It all depended on timing, but I knew I could do it.

The next day in our art class I switched art folders while Henry was up front, signing in for his presentation. It had been easier than I thought. Henry's folder was just lying there big as life on top of his desk, so I just switched folders as I walked by his desk.

I guess maybe I'm not really cut out for a life of crime because by the time I got back to my own desk, I was sweating bullets and I was sure my face was blazing like a three-alarm fire.

But Henry was still up front by the sign-in table, cool as a popsicle and laughing. I smiled to myself. I knew he wouldn't be laughing for long.

The next twenty minutes seemed to crawl by in slow motion while I waited for "H." H for Harrison.

Angela Carson talked about her charcoal sketches. It seemed like she was going to go on forever.

Then Michael Goodwin showed the class his watercolors while I watched the clock. Precious minutes were ticking by and the hairs on the back of my neck were beginning to tingle as I waited.

Then we finally got to "H"—time for Henry Harrison to meet his match.

I watched Henry strut to the front of the class with his folder under his arm. He announced that he would be talking about the photographs he had taken on our last field trip to the zoo. He stood there, just grinning at us, like he was going to blow us all away with his awesome photographs.

I peeked into his folder I had stashed in my desk. Sure enough, there were pages of photographs taken at the zoo—all neatly organized and labeled. I had to admit the photographs were good, really good.

I glanced up at Henry and watched his smile dim from one hundred watts to total blackout as he opened his folder and saw what was there. Nothing but blank paper!

He opened his mouth, but the only thing that came out was this funny little gurgle.

At last I had him right where I wanted him. Henry Harrison was about to find out what it felt like to be humiliated in front of the whole class.

I knew I could still give Henry's folder back to him and save the day for him or I could watch him self-destruct right in front of my eyes.

If you were Jeremy, what would *you* do? Why?

More to think about:

Do you think Jeremy should return Henry Harrison's folder to him? Why or why not?

Do you think Jeremy will really feel better if Henry Harrison is humiliated in front of the whole class? Why or why not?

Do you think Henry Harrison deserves to be humiliated?

Do you think it's okay to purposely hurt someone else if you think they deserve it? Why or why not?

When someone hurts you, do you think it's important to always "even the score"? Why or why not?

Not in a Zillion Years

Never, never, never! I will never forgive her. Not in a million years. Not in a zillion years!

I locked the bathroom door and slumped down on the edge of the bathtub. I stared at the piece of paper in my hand—the list of the roles for our school play, *Beauty and the Beast*.

I had tried out for the part of Belle and I wanted that part more than anything. But my name, Shawna Mitchell, wasn't there. My name was way down the list next to "townspeople."

Erica's name was at the top of the list next to "Belle," the place where mine should have been.

Erica, my best friend. She hadn't even planned to try out. She just tagged along with me for kicks. And then, at the last minute, she tried out on a dare.

Alex dared her to try out. And she did. Just like that. That was Erica. She wasn't afraid of anything. Just dare her to do something—anything— and she'd do it.

So she tried out and she got the part. *My* part. I will never forgive her as long as I live. I ripped the paper into tiny pieces and flushed them down the toilet. I watched them swirl around in the whirlpool of water. Going, going, gone! Just like our friendship. I would never speak to Erica again. Ever.

I slammed the bathroom door behind me and headed out to the kitchen to get myself some comfort food.

As I poured the milk, I began to simmer down a little, but I couldn't get Erica out of my head. There she was, dressed in Belle's gold gown. *My* gown. And dancing with the beast.

But as I finished off the last of the peanut butter in the jar, more images forced their way into my brain and into my heart.

Images of Erica bringing my homework to me every day last year when I was home with the flu for a whole week. And Erica inviting me to go to the Sahuaro Ranch last summer with her and her family. A vacation at a real ranch with a horse of my very own for the entire week. I would remember that incredible week for the rest of my life.

And as I drank my milk to wash down the peanut butter that was stuck in my throat, I remembered last Tuesday in the cafeteria. And Peter. Peter was forever making jokes about my braces. I was used to him calling me "metal-mouth" and "zipper-lips," but lately he had started calling me "mush-mouth" and imitating what he called my "lispth."

Last Tuesday in the school lunchroom will be burned into my memory bank forever. Peter was two tables away, but I could still hear him sounding off about my braces and imitating my "lispth." I could feel my head getting hotter while imaginary steam shot out of my ears. I just wanted to evaporate into thin air and disappear forever.

But Erica, who was sitting next to me, didn't even break a sweat. Her eyes just lit up in this special way which is usually a dangerous sign, and that's when she did it.

She picked up her paper cup of raisins and hurled them across both tables right at Peter. He ducked for cover when he saw the raisins coming, but it was still a bull's-eye for Erica.

I couldn't help but smile as I replayed the video. One minute, Peter was wisecracking like he was king of the hill and the next minute he was ducking for cover like he was being bombarded by rockets.

Erica got twenty demerits for that little incident, but she told me it was worth it because it was for a good cause. The cause of friendship. And then she gave me this huge hug.

That moment I knew we would be best friends forever. And I really believed that. Until today!

Now I wasn't so sure I could ever forgive Erica for what she had done to me.

If you were Shawna, what would *you* do? Why?

More to think about:

Do you think Erica tried to hurt Shawna deliberately?

Can friends sometimes unintentionally hurt each other? Do you think Shawna should forgive Erica? Why or why not?

Can real friends be honest with each other?

Do you think Erica is a good friend? Why or why not?

The Disagreeable Dare

"I can't believe you did that," I said, squeezing my eyes shut to show my disgust. "That is so gross. Whoever heard of peanut butter on a hot dog? You're lucky you didn't throw up all over the table."

Emilio grinned one of his huge grins and shoved the empty mustard jar across the table to me. "You were out of mustard, so I had to use my imagination. A little catsup, a little mayo, and a lot of peanut butter and jelly. Don't knock it till you've tried it."

I watched him wipe his mouth with his sleeve while I tried to keep from barfing.

Then he let loose with another huge grin. "So what are you going to do? Are you going to do it or not?"

I didn't have a clue what he was talking about, so I just grinned back at him. "I don't know. Do you think I should?"

"Samantha, sometimes you are such a pain. You weren't even listening, were you?"

When Emilio calls me "Samantha," I know he's really upset, so I shook my head and tried to look contrite.

"I guess not. I was just thinking about Diana and her dumb challenge."

"Earth-to-Samantha. That's just who I was talking about before you zoned out on me. So what are you going to do?"

I replayed the video from last Friday in my head. There I was standing in line in the lunchroom minding my own business when Diana and her friend Carly shove their way into line behind me. And then in front of the whole world Diana says, "I hear you're the big karate champ around this place, but you don't look so tough to me. I bet I could beat you with one hand tied behind my back."

The lunchroom gets so quiet you could hear a popsicle melt, and I can feel everyone's eyes glued on me, waiting for me to say something brilliant.

My mouth feels like it's stuffed with my mom's whole jar of cotton balls and it feels like my brain has suddenly shut down.

Now Diana moves so close that she's practically hovering over me. "So what do you say, Champ? How about a little sparring match in the gym after school on Monday to see who the real champ is around here?"

Then Carly adds her two cents. "Maybe you should back off, Diana. Can't you see she's so scared she can't talk?"

And that's when Diana announces in a voice loud enough for the whole world to hear, "I'll see you in the gym Monday afternoon or else!"

As I replay the events from last Friday, I can feel my stomach tightening up all over again.

Then Emilio's voice interrupts the video rolling through my head and brings it to a screeching halt. "Sam, you know you could take her easy, she's only a purple belt. You're a brown belt and you'll be testing for your black belt this spring."

I shake my head and stare at the empty mustard jar in front of me. "That's not the point. I probably could win, but I don't want to fight her just to prove something. I don't feel I have anything to prove."

Emilio stops chewing and he's no longer smiling. "You know she's not going to get off your case till you fight her. I don't see that you have much choice here."

I know Emilio's trying to help, but he's not the one with the problem. It's my problem and I'm the one who's going to have to figure out what to do about it.

But Emilio is still trying. "She doesn't go to your karate school, but maybe we could set up a sparring match at your school and your karate instructor would agree to be the judge."

I shake my head again. "I don't think Mr. Cameron would go for that. He's always telling us to use our karate skills only when necessary and never to show off."

If you were Sam, what would *you* do? Why?

More to think about:

Why do you think Diana has challenged Sam?

Would you consider Diana a bully? Why or why not?

Do you know someone like Diana?

Which do you think would take more courage: to accept the dare or to ignore the dare? Why?

When other people are telling you what to do, how do you decide what is right for you?

Nothing Is Forever

I am such a loser! I can't even tell a curveball from a fastball. Yesterday I ducked out of the way because I thought the ball was coming right at me and then, at the last minute, it broke sharply over the plate for a strike. Boy, did I feel dumb.

So today I see this ball that looks like it's coming right at me again, and I hold my ground. But this time it doesn't break and it crashes right into my shoulder. Talk about bad days!

Maybe it's my eyes. And then again, maybe not. Maybe it's all my body parts! They just don't seem to work together the way they're supposed to.

Last week I was playing right field and there's this perfect fly ball. I keep my eye on the ball the whole time it's coming down and—plunk!—there it is right in my glove. And then it rolls out! I still can't believe it. The ball is right there in my glove and then I lose it.

I know one thing for sure. And that's that I, Corey Adams, will not be signing up for the baseball league this summer.

And did I mention the fact that I'm also "vertically challenged"? In other words, I'm short. I've been the shortest kid in my class every year for just about as long as I can remember. And I'm the shortest kid again this year.

Do you want a sneak preview of the coming year? Okay, the first day of school I'll get stuck in the front row again, so that I can see the blackboard. I never get to sit in the back rows where all the action is.

And then there's my gym class when we're choosing teams for basketball. Guess who's always the last guy picked!

I could go on forever, but you're probably getting the picture by now. I've been clobbered with all this bad stuff while everyone else in the world gets loaded up with all the good stuff. It's just not fair.

As I'm trying to cram all my stuff into my locker, Steven rolls by in his wheelchair with his saxophone in his lap. He's probably going to be in that wheelchair for the rest of his life because of a diving accident last year.

He used to be a basketball star and I bet he could have ended up being a professional basketball player because he was really good. So much for his glory days!

Now he's joined some wheelchair basketball group that goes around to different schools doing exhibition games to show kids that a physical disability doesn't have to wreck your life. Yeah, right! Like his life isn't wrecked!

Steven slaps me a high five as he rolls by and reminds me about band practice. I was going to join band again this year, but now I'm not so sure.

I love playing the clarinet, but some of the other kids play better than I do, so I'm not sure I want to sign up again this year. Besides, I'm not sure I want to spend hours glued to a clarinet when I could be watching TV or playing video games.

As I'm passing by the gym later that afternoon, I hear someone bouncing a ball, so I crack open the door to check out who's in there.

I should have guessed. It's Steven practicing his free throws. That guy never gives up. He's always saying that he's going to keep practicing his free throws till he's as good as he was before the accident.

He's always saying stuff like that. Like there's no such thing as a loser, and that you're only a loser if you give up and don't try.

I guess if I practiced my clarinet as much as he practices his free throws, I'd be pretty good, too. Maybe I'll think about signing up for band again, and then again maybe not.

If you were Corey, what would *you* do? Why?

More to think about:

Do you think Corey has really been stuck with all the "bad stuff"?

How do you think Steven is handling his disability?

Who do you think has a better attitude—Corey or Steven? Why?

Do you think Steven will reach his goal? Why or why not?

Who do you think is going to end up more successful in life? Why?

To Puff or Not to Puff

I'm always telling my friends how cool my mom is. She's not afraid of spiders or snakes. She actually likes my white rats and she's really great at cleaning up dog puke.

I figured that's why Melanie voted to have the overnight at my house. Because she liked my mom. Boy, was I wrong!

Friday night my overnight starts out really great. We're all pigging out on our triple-cheese pizza and watching videos. Then at the stroke of midnight my party suddenly becomes X-rated.

That's when Melanie disappears into the bathroom with her backpack. When she comes out, she's grinning like the cat who just swallowed the canary and holding a marijuana cigarette.

Now I know why Melanie wanted the overnight at my house. Because my bedroom is down on the lower level next to the laundry room. And away from everyone else in the house.

So, anyway, Melanie plops down on the rug and holds the cigarette up like it's some kind of trophy. "Look what I swiped out of my brother's desk. He won't even miss it and we can have our own special little party. This will really be a night to remember!"

In less than a nanosecond all the girls have formed a circle around her, ready to join her party. I'm still standing there watching my friends, wishing I could get out of there and go home. But I *am* home and my party is suddenly Melanie's party and out of my control.

I watch Melanie light the cigarette and take a puff. She rolls her eyes dramatically and makes a really big deal out of it. Then she passes it on to Neda with a flourish like she's passing on the Holy Grail.

I can tell that Neda can hardly wait for her turn. She's always ready to try anything. I watch her take a puff and pass it on.

When it gets to Gina, I see her hesitate and I know exactly what's going through her mind. She's always telling me you've got "to go along to get along" and I know she's going to end up taking a puff even if she doesn't really want to.

By the time the cigarette makes it back to Melanie, everyone has had a turn. Everyone but me.

I'm still standing there watching everything like it's a foreign film with subtitles I don't understand. I've never even smoked a regular cigarette and I'm not about to puff on marijuana just because everyone else is doing it.

But right now all my friends are staring at me, waiting for me to take my turn.

"Here, Tracy," Melanie says, holding the cigarette out to me, while different escape scenarios roll through my head.

I know I can pretend to take a puff, but that wouldn't be the honest thing to do. I tell myself that I should either take a real puff like all the others or else just come right out and refuse to do it.

Yeah, right! That would go over like a lead balloon. That would be the end of my social life for the rest of the year, maybe for the rest of my life. These are my best friends, the kids I hang out with every day. And I could end up losing them just like that.

Then I tell myself that one little puff isn't going to do any real harm. That would be the easy way out and I never claimed to be any superhero.

I know what I want to do, but I'm not sure I can do it. The stakes here are pretty high: If I don't take a puff, I lose all my friends, but if I do take a puff, how will I feel about myself?

If you were Tracy, what would *you* do? Why?

More to think about:

Why do you think Tracy doesn't want to smoke the cigarette?

What do you think will happen if Tracy doesn't take her turn?

Do you think she will really lose all her friends?

Do you think everyone there really wants to take a turn? Why or why not?

Do you think it will take more courage for Tracy to smoke the cigarette or not smoke it? Why?

What do you do when your friends try to get you to do something you don't want to do?

Willaby, Werewolves, and Worms

My name is Brian and, ever since the big "D," my whole world has been turned upside down. I have so many mixed-up feelings boiling up inside me that sometimes I feel like I'm going to explode and everything will come spurting out of me, just like the cotton stuffing in my cousin's rag doll.

My whole world self-destructed with no warning at all. One morning we're all eating breakfast together and the next morning, my dad's moving into his own apartment and it's just Mom and me.

It's like one day I have one kind of life and the very next day I've got a whole different kind of life.

I'm beginning to develop a split personality because I have two homes, two bedrooms, two lives.

When I'm with my dad at his apartment, sometimes I want to work on one of my model planes, only it's at my mom's house. And then when I'm with my mom and I want to finish a book I'm reading, I remember it's at my dad's apartment.

Living in two places is a real pain! When I'm with my dad I get homesick for my mom, and when I'm with my mom I get homesick for my dad.

And then there are stepparents. You hear stories all the time about the evil stepmother, but no one ever warns you about the evil stepdad. In this case, his name is Kevin.

We have a Father-Son banquet coming up at school and my real dad can't go, but there's no way I'm inviting Kevin.

Friday nights my real dad and I used to watch monster movies together while we pigged out on junk food. I don't think Kevin has ever watched a horror flick in his whole life.

And my real dad and I used to go fishing just about every Saturday during the summer. I bet Kevin doesn't even know how to dig for worms in the backyard or bait a hook.

And my dog, Willaby, always went fishing with us. Speaking of dogs, Kevin has never even owned a dog in his whole entire life, which may explain why he's so weird.

Now, Willaby weighs in at over a hundred pounds, and to be honest, I think Kevin's a little scared of him.

Tonight is Friday night, movie and pizza night, so Kevin is over at the video store picking out tonight's entertainment.

He always rents three movies at a time and last week he brought back three videos about animal habitats. Maybe this time he'll bring back something really exciting like *The Migration Habits of the Wild Boar*.

Well, anyway, now you understand why I'm in such a funk!

My parents do this whole divorce thing all on their own, but it's me who ends up with the wicked stepfather and a split personality.

It sounds like Kevin's back and there's the video bag right on the dining room table where he always leaves everything. I think I'll just take one little peek in the bag while he's in the kitchen with Mom. Then I'll know whether I should come down with the flu, so I can go to my room and watch some decent TV shows.

Well, whoopee doo! I told you! Three videos. I can predict everything this guy does, right down to the color of his socks.

So let's see what we have here. I don't believe this! I totally don't believe this! *The Werewolf Trilogy*! This will most definitely drive my mom wild—she hates horror films.

And what's this under the bag? Kevin must have stopped at the pet store too because there's a huge rawhide bone for Willaby. Good grief, it must be two feet long. It'll take him forever to chew that thing.

Just maybe Kevin isn't a total loser after all. I wonder if maybe I should reconsider inviting him to the Father-Son banquet.

If you were Brian, what would you do? Why?

More to think about:

Can you understand how Brian feels about his real dad?

Can you understand why he feels the way he does about Kevin?

Do you think Brian is treating Kevin fairly? Why or why not?

How do you think Kevin is feeling?

Do you think Kevin's mom knows how Kevin feels?

Do you think Brian can be nice to Kevin without being disloyal to his real dad? Why or why not?

Operation Stephanie

"Quick, hide, or she'll see you," Laurie whispered, pulling Jenna down beside her behind the dumpster.

The girls shot each other a thumbs-up as Stephanie passed by without seeing them.

Laurie stood up and readjusted her backpack. "You know, Jen, I don't think I could have listened to one more word from that girl without totally losing it."

"Me either," Jenna agreed, as both girls headed off across the street toward the local shopping mall.

"Do you know how many times Stephanie has told me about her family's new swimming pool, their new camper, and her own private telephone?" Laurie muttered as she quickened her pace.

"You forgot her brother's new sports car," Jenna added.

Laurie nodded. "Yeah, yeah, I know. Listen, I hear all that stuff every day of my life in math class and then again in Spanish class. It's like a never-ending soap opera: the life and times of Stephanie and her entire family."

"It's no wonder she doesn't have any friends," Jenna grumbled as she stuffed her hands deeper into the pockets of her windbreaker and quickened her own pace to keep up with her friend. "I'm just glad I lucked out and don't have her in any of my classes this year."

"You know what she probably does when she's alone?" Laurie mused. "I can see it all now in living color. She stands in front of her mirror telling it how wonderful she is."

Jenna smiled as she, too, let her imagination run wild. "Yeah, I see it now. Stephanie talking to her only friend—her mirror. And then suddenly the mirror cracks right down the middle. After all, how much can it take? Even a mirror is bound to crack up some day if it spends too much time with Stephanie."

Both girls burst into hysterical laughter and had to stop walking as their friend Amanda caught up with them.

"So what's going on with you guys?"

"Jenna rolled her eyes and grinned. "We just escaped before Stephanie Wilson trapped us with more tales of her illustrious family."

Amanda shook her head. "I don't think she's all that bad. Maybe just a little insecure and shy."

"Yeah, right!" Laurie exclaimed, scrunching up her face. "If she's insecure, then I should be so insecure with all the junk she's got."

"Give me a break!" Jenna muttered in exasperation. "She's a creep.

You know she's a creep, we know she's a creep. The whole world knows she's a creep."

"But just think about it for a minute," Amanda protested. "How would you feel if you didn't have any friends and everyone tried to avoid you? Wouldn't you feel a little desperate, too?"

"Hang on a minute," Laurie interrupted. "Don't you have things a little backward here? Stephanie doesn't have any friends because she's so totally boring, stuck-up, and obnoxious, not the other way around."

"Okay, okay, but it still turns out the same either way," Amanda persisted. "She still doesn't have any friends because she's driving them all away. I think we should talk to her about it."

"Yeah, right! And just who's going to do that?" Jenna asked, glaring at Amanda.

Amanda smiled. "Wait a minute, I think I've got an even better idea. Let's make Stephanie our secret project and see if we can get through to her by being nice to her. We could even begin by inviting her to our sleepover Friday night."

Jenna shook her head. "I think it's a dumb idea, but it would be a real test for us to see if we can actually be nice to someone who's so totally obnoxious. How about it Laurie, are you in or not?"

If you were Laurie, what would *you* do? Why?

More to think about:

Why do you think Stephanie brags so much?

Do you think it's okay to treat Stephanie the way Laurie and Jenna are treating her? Why or why not?

How do you think Stephanie will feel if she finds out that Laurie and Jenna are purposely avoiding her?

Do you think Amanda might be right about Stephanie?

What do you think of Amanda's plan?

Do you think Amanda's plan might work? Why or why not?

Critical Choice

"You are such a dork, Shannon! Sometimes I don't know why I even hang out with you."

Shannon stopped inhaling her chocolate malt and looked up. "Chill out, Kelsey. I didn't say I wouldn't do it. I just said I wanted to think about it."

Kelsey stared at the menu in front of her. "So what's there to think about? It's not like we're robbing a bank or anything."

Shannon took the straw out of her malt and let the malt dribble through the straw onto her tongue. "I know that, but it's still cheating."

Kelsey slammed her menu down on the table and eyeballed Shannon. "So what's the big deal, anyway? All you have to do is sign my mother's name to my summer reading list and I sign your mom's name to your summer reading list. No one will ever know we didn't really read the books and that way we can get a free book from the bookstore."

Kelsey rummaged through her backpack until she found a yellow flyer. "See, here it is."

READ 8 BOOKS.

Have your parent sign this slip that you have read the 8 books. Then bring the signed slip back to us and pick a FREE BOOK from the special table at the front of the store. The FREE BOOK is yours to keep. HAPPY READING!

Kelsey shoved the flyer across the table and Shannon read through it again. Then she shook her head. "I just don't think it's right. The bookstore is going to give us a free book for reading eight books and they're expecting us to be honest about it. It's like a promise that we've really read those books. So why don't we just read the eight books? Then we won't have to cheat to get the free book."

Kelsey grabbed the flyer and stuffed it into her backpack. "So who has time to read eight books? I don't know about you, but I plan to spend my summer hanging out with the gang at the lake."

"But we could read at the lake and still hang out with the gang at the same time."

Kelsey screwed up her face and groaned. "Yeah, right. I can just see it now. I'm water skiing with the rope in one hand and a book in the other hand. Get real, Shannon."

Shannon could feel her face burn. "You know what I mean. We don't spend all of our time on water skis. We could easily read a book a week while we're at the lake."

Kelsey groaned again. "Grow up, Shannon. Don't you get it? I don't want to read eight books. I don't want to read *any* books. I want to have some fun this summer."

Shannon shook her head again. "I just don't know. I need some time to think about it."

Kelsey grabbed her backpack and stood up. "You want time? I'll give you time. I'll give you all summer to get your act together. I don't know what's happened to you. Last year you would have gone along with this without even thinking twice about it. Now you're getting to be a real pain."

Then she marched over to the cashier, paid her bill, and stormed out of the malt shop.

Shannon sat in the booth doing a quick rerun of what had just happened. So what had she said to make Kelsey flip out like that? She only wanted to do what was right. What was so wrong with that?

It looked like a lose-lose situation. Go along with Kelsey and keep a friend by doing something dishonest or refuse to go along with her and lose a friend. Her best friend. Not an easy choice.

If you were Shannon, what would *you* do? Why?

More to think about:

Why do you think Shannon doesn't want to go along with Kelsey?

How do you think Shannon will feel if she does go along? Why?

Why do you think Kelsey feels that Shannon should go along with her plan to get a free book?

Why do you think Kelsey is so angry at Shannon?

Do you think Kelsey is a good friend? Why or why not?

What do you do when you have a "lose-lose" situation like this?